Fortune Cookies

Volume 9

Dr. Kareem Pottinger

YSD Publishing House

Library of Congress Catalog in
Publication Data

YSD PUBLISHING HOUSE
14490 Coastal Bay Circle 13204
Naples, FL. 34119

Library of Congress Catalog Card
Number:
2013934185
International Standard Book
Number 978-1-937171-08-7

Dedicated to my firstborn

YOUNGSABATH POTTINGER

If I ever leave this planet, I have
always kept you in mind.

Not leavening my wisdom far behind

Grow Good

INTRODUCTION

The true intent of this book
was to write a set of guidelines
that could be
immediately implemented in
the progress and advancement
of my sons elite
life.
This vast deep knowledge was
to be used as a
tool
to keep him far beyond just,
"ahead of the learning curb" for
lack of better expression.
These
rules are the widely accepted
and used unspoken
secrets amongst the elite in
which we use to rear our

young.
Although these are our
secrets
and most of us will and should
be extremely displeased for
having them on display for the
"normal's" of the world to
receive, I decided to release
them nevertheless.
For,
upon reading the finished
piece I realized that these elite
secrets
could not only serve to benefit
my son and family to come
well, but that the entire
world
could serve to benefit from
these lists of guidelines.
The way that this book is
intended to be received is to

ponder upon each page for a complete 24 hours.

Each page is to be pondered upon for the whole day; it is to be used as topic of discussion for that day amongst peers, friends, and family members' etcetera.

It is especially designed to be pondered upon mostly by you. For a complete 24 hours deep thought on each subject should be pondered upon. The reason being is to see how these guidelines could be implemented into your current life, how should they have been implemented in your past life, and how can they benefit your future.

It
is only through the true
belief
and usage of these
guidelines
that your life's
works will be greatly
affected
in its progress.

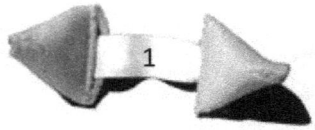

No-one
is
completely
content,
except
for
the
losers
of
the
world

*It is important
to realize that
to
always have a
true-friend
is a
wonderful-gift
sent-down
to
you from
the
universe*

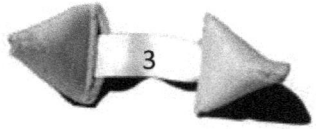

*Whenever
you are willing
to get together
with other
people, you
have to
accept
the fact
that
people
are
different*

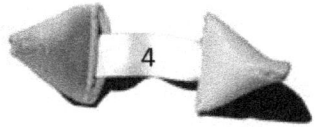

A
gift
is a
way
to keep
that
day,
that very
hour
stuck-fast
into
time

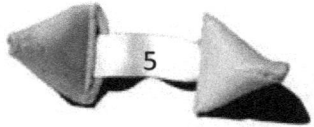

*In life you have
to figure-out
what you need
to do in order to
get
where you
want to go and
then, do what
you can in
order to get
what you need
accomplished*

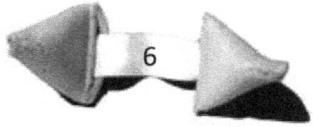

*It takes
a
strong-sense
of
character
to be yourself
and not what
other
people would
like, want, or
think you
should be*

The bitter-fruits of betrayal must be plucked from your fire immediately or else it will begin to dampen your flame

*Don't
ever
allow
another
person
to
take
away
from
your
happiness*

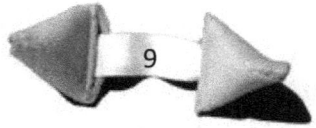

Sometimes for your cause; all you will have to do in order to complete it is, to continue what you are doing, bide-your-time, and hold-out for hope to take-root

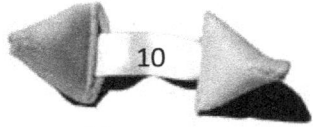

*When dealing
with people,
you should
always
remember that
there
isn't
anything
as
inconsistent
as the
human-heart*

When
you are
not
prepared,
life
comes
at
you quick
and
passes
by
you fast

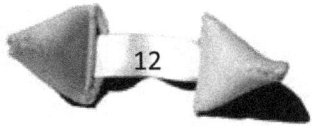

In life you will
always
have
to
keep-up
with
the
times
or
you will
fall
behind

In life you should want to make something substantial of yourself, do not pout around in slow-crawl with no destination at all

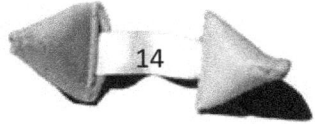

*With
each
new-day
there
will
always
be
a
possibility
for
a
new-way*

15

Your main-job
in life
should always
be
to
clear your path
with light
and
success
for
the
future

You cannot fight against the destiny that you have set in motion for yourself

*The people who
are in your life
that are
insincere
will always
be
smitten-out
of
your life
by
the strong-hand
of the
universe*

*Love
for-self
is
the
only
kind of love
that
exist
within
the
privileged
class*

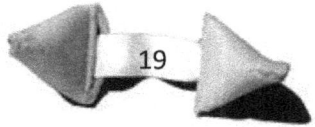

*Aristocrats
do not
bother with
hassles such
as
money, this is
something
that you need
to keep in mind
when dealing
with the
privileged-class*

*Regardless
of the
many different
circumstances
that you may
find yourself in;
whether good
or bad
you should
always insist
on room for
hope*

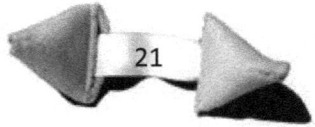

*A
human-being
without
secrets
does
not
exist*

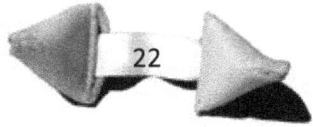

*The only person
in
this world
that
you
are
suppose
to
count
on
is
yourself*

*There is no
reason
to swear
loyalty to the
people
who will not
extend
their
hand-out
to
protect
you*

In regards to dealing with you and accomplishing your goals, there should be no such thing as borders or boundaries

*Keep in mind
that in
the process
of traveling
many different
foreign-worlds
you will become
tainted
by the
divers-customs
of
those worlds*

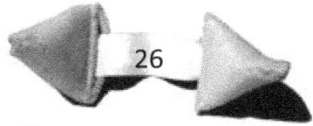

*In the fate
that
you have
created
for
yourself it is
very important
for you to
realize that
there are
no
coincidences*

In life you should always try to the utmost to play your situations correctly

or

be prepared to suffer the consequences

*Sometimes the main
and only problem that
you might have
is that you are
doing good
when the
effort
requires for
you to be doing
great*

*To be
completely
committed
and never
questioning
yourself
will be the
only
way for you to
perform
at your
best*

*It is all about
making the best
out of every
aspect of your
life;
this is what is
required,
to be
consistently
performing at
your
optimum-level*

*Understand
that when two
people
have feelings
for
one-another,
there is
nothing that
anyone
can do
to
stop-it*

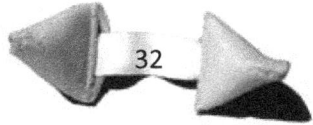

*There should be
only one speed
and
direction
that
your life should
always be
moving in and
that is at
pace
and
forward*

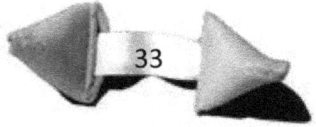

*After placing
the
initial-effort
towards your
goal
you have to be
prepared to do
whatever it
takes to protect
the
investments
of those efforts*

*You
have to be
willing
to give your
all
or else
you're
wasting
everyone else's
time
including your
own*

*Be aware that
a lot of the
times when
the facts
do not
go with what
people say, that
some of those
people will
change
the
facts*

What
a
person
is
to
be
they
are
now
becoming,
pay
attention

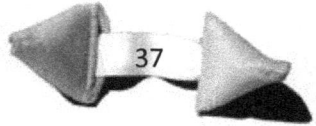

When
you
come
with
the
least
you
should
always
give
the
most

You should always treat people well in life because the person you get rid-of could be the very person too give you your next opportunity

*For
the
right
price
everything
is
for
sale*

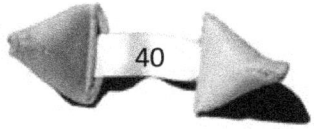

*Untended
love
could
mean
nothing
but
trouble,
so
be
careful*

Curiosity
is
a
sure
sign
of
intelligence

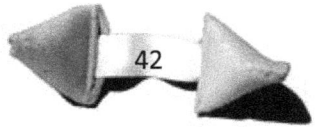

You can not
get
mad
at
a
bull
when
it
gives
you
the
horns

Pay absolute attention to your inside voice because as your intuition becomes stronger and stronger so will your path become clearer and clearer

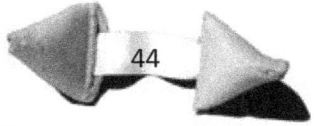

With
control;
you don't
realize
how
little you have
until
you
have
none
at
all

Your intuition is your path and the sooner that you understand this the sooner you will realize that your map is inside you

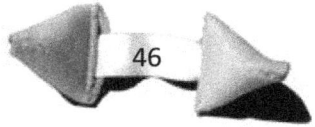

Only

a

winner

goes

the

extra

mile

in

order

to

make

it

*In
order
to succeed
you have
to have the
skill,
the will,
the
want,
and
the
heart*

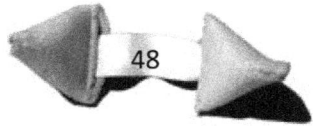

*Be
prepared
to ask yourself
how
far are
you willing
to
go
in
order
to
succeed*

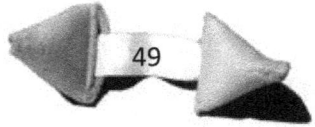

Your talent will
never become
or
mean
anything
unless you
work at
it
and
then
use
it

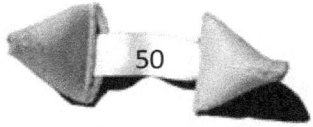

Everybody
has
a
skeleton or two
in
their
closet,
everyone
on
this
planet
does

Be careful of thinking that you are moving forward when you are actually taking two-steps backwards

Whatever you are doing just make sure that it is working towards where you want to be

*True
effort
is
always
harder
before
it
gets
easier*

*Never
feel the
need
to
poke
your
nose
in
someone
else's
family
affair*

*In
life
you
should
always
want
to
evolve*

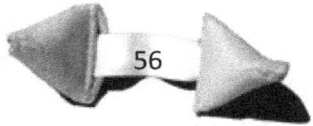

*Before you
speak, you
should always
keep in mind
and know
whether you
care or not that
some people
might get
offended
if you say
what you feel*

*Do not be
dismayed
by the
illusion
of
boundaries;
for there is no
such thing in
life, there
are
only
possibilities*

*When you
acquire a
partner
or
get involved
with one,
it is
important
to make
sure that their
goal matches
your goal*

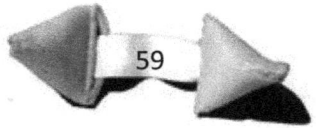

*You
should
always
pay
attention
to
the
details*

*People
cannot
just
fall-out
of
love,
there
are
always
reasoning's
behind
it*

Anything
that
is
not
moving
forward
in
life
is
moving
backwards

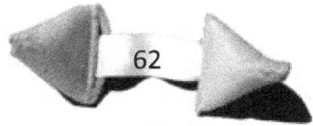

It is extremely important to understand that it is very rare in life to receive a true-friend and that not all the people that you consider your friend is your true-friend

*As long as that
you
are
heading
in the
right-direction,
things do not
have
to be what you
consider
to be
perfect*

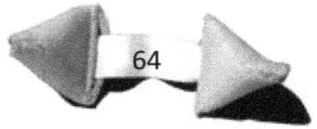

*You
have
to
spend
some
money
in order
to
bring about
some
money*

*In
life
one-day
you
have it
and
the
next-day
you don't,
it is just how
it
goes*

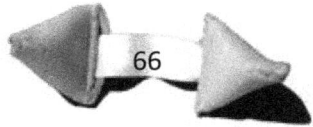

*Feelings
of love
and
feelings
of hate
both
start of
as
caring
deeply
for
someone*

67

*In life it is very
important
to get
your
perspective
by
looking
at things
from the
sides
that
matter*

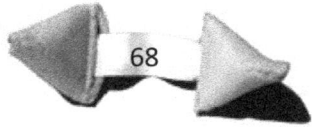

It is very important to understand that when you are failing in a particular aim, a lot of the times it is because of the decisions that you are making

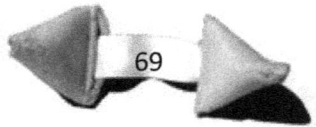

*Your future is
constantly
changing
for the better
or
the worst
depending
upon the
decisions that
you are
currently
making*

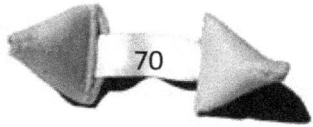

*You
have
to
think
big
in
order
to
accomplish
big*

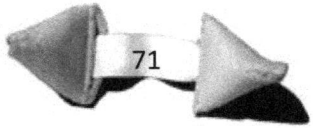

*Timing
means
absolutely
everything;
the
right
place
at
the
right
time*

*Always
remember that
the most
important
thing
in
everything
that
you
do
is
you*

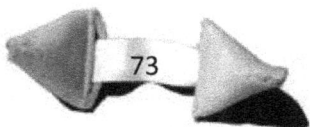

It doesn't matter
the
time
nor
the
place
you
should
never
give-up
on
your dreams

If you're not careful,
you will always
end-up
with the type
of person
you
never
expected
to
be
with

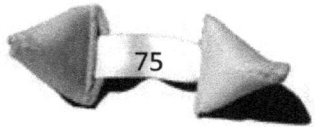

There are many different ways to make it in this world, do not get locked into one-view

*Every
time that there
is a
struggle in your
life,
it is to
prepare
you
for what
is
to
come*

*Only
the
truth
will
allow
you
to
evolve*

*Don't
ask
for
something
that
befits
a
burden
when
you
receive
it*

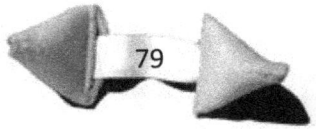

*A person's
initial
reaction
is
always
the
absolute-truth
of how
they
really feel,
so
pay attention*

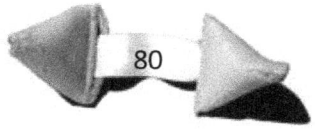

Relationships
need
time
invested

*If
you do not
take no for an
answer,
with enough
effort
eventually
the
answer
will
come back
as a yes*

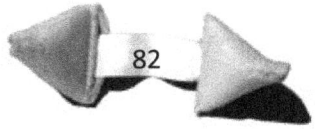

*For anything
that you
truly
want to
receive,
you should
never
give-up
putting-effort
in it
until you
receive-it*

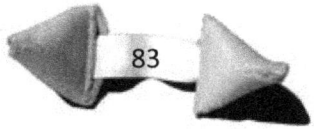

The
true-question
in every
conflict
is what has
been
lost
and
what
has
been
gained

You should always fight for what you believe in

When a persons inhibitions are down, that person displays their truest of feelings

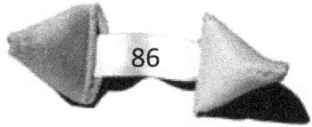

*A
winners
principles
are
to
never
give-up,
never
let-down,
and
never
forget*

*In
order
to
truly
succeed
you have
to be
prepared
to give
anything
at
anytime*

*Always
remember that
any person
can have an
accusation
thrown
at
them,
it does not
mean that the
accusation is
true*

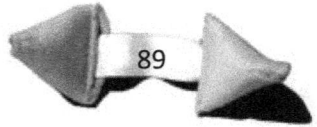

The
contempt
for
money
is a trick
from the rich
to
keep
the
poor
without
it

*When
you want
to thank
someone,
make sure
it is
a
person
that
deserves
your
thanks*

*It
is important for
you to realize
that it is a
great-gift
to be
in
a
position
to make
a
difference*

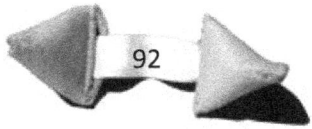

*It
should
be very
infrequent
in
life
that you
should
want
to
take
long-shots*

*Continuous
persistence
is
one
of
the
keys
to
success*

*Starting from
the
bottom
and going to
the
top
is
how you will
gain the
complete
understanding
of things*

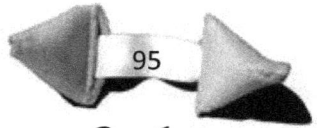

Be aware of the fact that there will always be someone in life who would like to take your-spot

*When
situations
get
complicated,
you
just
have to
make the
most
of
what
you have*

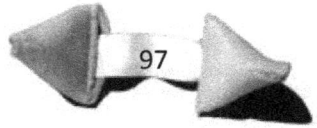

*When someone
has paid for
your talent
and
you do not
perform
to their
liking,
expect
to
get
traded*

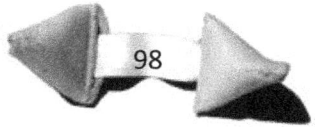

*You
cannot
buy
true-acceptance*

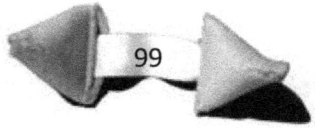

*As
your
career
moves
forward,
you
should
always
refocus*

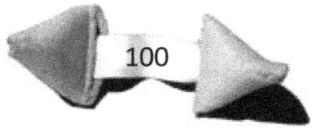

Talent
means nothing
in a game
that you
need
to
be
careful
and
have
discipline
in

It is only when
you think
that you
are
worth
the
best
that you
will
always
want the
best

102

*Self-
examination
is a
critical part
of
maturity
so
make sure
that you
are constantly
doing
it*

*Money
doesn't always
buy
you happiness,
it is
what you do
with the
money
that may bring
you
closer
to it*

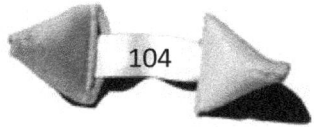

*It
only
takes
a
minor
deviation
to
create
a
major
change*

*If
you
don't
try
for
yourself,
you will
never
truly
know
for
yourself*

*When
you are
not
prepared,
opportunity
disappears
before
you can
even
try
and
stop-it*

*You
have to
take
your
chances
when
you
can,
otherwise
you
will
regret-it*

*The spot
that you
earn
in
this
world
will be
a
direct-result
of
your
efforts*

*Never
make
light
of
an
opportunity
when
presented*

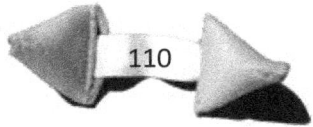

*Just
because
a
person
is
young
does not
mean
that
person
is
inexperienced*

*You should
never
allow
another
person
to
keep
you
from
living
your
life*

In life in order
to
make
room for
new-things
you will have to
sometimes
get
rid-of
a
few
old-things

113

In life you should never want to get yourself involved in another person's misery

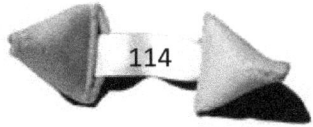

*Great
things
happen
to
determined
people*

*Unless
they
are for
some
higher
purpose,
deeds
in it of
themselves
are
meaning
less*

In a world of appearances; it is not really about what you are, it's about what people think you are

*The only way
for you to
completely
understand
what and
where
the
line
is,
is for you
to
cross-it*

*Never
turn
down
an
opportunity
to
learn
from
the
source*

Sometimes
you will
have
to
bend
with
the
breeze
or
break
against
it

It is
very
important
to
understand
that
in
life,
each-task
has
its
season

*Do
not
muddy
the
present
with
the
past*

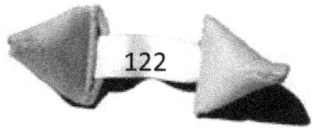

*Beware,
things
are
rarely
as
simple
as
they
seem*

How are you getting towards a happier-place, this is a question that needs to always remain in the back of your mind

*When
it's
about
business
you
cannot
get attached
to
anyone
or
anything*

*Keep in mind
that
everything
"looks"
easy
when
it's
been
done
a
thousand
times*

*In
whatever
it is
that
you
do,
you
have
to
stay
in
perspective*

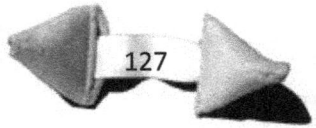

For the thinking person; no matter how bad the situation a way-out can always be made

Letting
people
earn
their
own
stripes
is
what
is
best
for
all

*You must
continuously
move-on
and
upwards
throughout
your life
in
order
to
achieve
success*

One of the best things you could ever learn how to do, is to learn how to be quite

*When
people
grab
without
thinking
it
is
because
they
are
passionate
about it*

*In regards to
building
trust
with people;
going fast
is
slow,
and
going
slow
is
fast*

*It is all about
illusions,
how
you
appear
to be
to the outside
world is
exactly how
the outside
world will treat
you*

*Start
with this
and
then you move
on to the
next,
this is how
you
build
a
proper
foundation*

*Without the
proper
maintenance
and
upkeep
any success
that you will
ever
establish
will always
be
fragile*

*Sometimes
a
person
has to be
big
enough
in order
to see
how small
they
really
are*

*What else
should you be
in life but
true to your
cause
and
faithful
to the
destiny in
which you have
created for
yourself*

Most people in this world like their life when it is full of simple things, they do not want to accomplish great things because it takes to much effort; adapt not one of these people's traits

*Trust
nothing
that
you
cannot
verify
for
yourself*

*If
you want to
learn
anything
about the world
you must
learn
the
patience
to
seek
it*

*Without
trust
there
can
be
no
betrayal*

The

more

you

see

the

more

you

will

learn

Trying to receive more by holding on to things will only cause stagnation; the universe has plenty to give in which you will receive only if you learn to let go

Where you stand in life depends a lot on where you are sitting

*Do
things
in the
correct
order
and you
will not
have
to
do
them
over*

If you would like to become great in life you must chart your own course, never leave it up to someone else to chart your course for you

To never let
yourself
down
is
the only
way
to get
to
where
you want
to go in
life

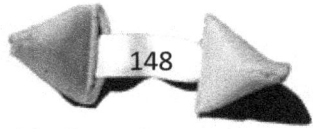

In your life in order to be someone substantial you must have a set of rules and goals, no set of rules and goals means no substantial future

*Too much of the
very same
thing that
brought
you up
can definitely
bring you
down, you have
to know when
enough
is
enough*

The world is yours, don't sleep

*Any
right
worth
having
is
a
right
worth
sacrificing
for*

*Anything
worth
doing
is
worth
doing
with
excellence*

*Your
timing
is
absolutely
everything*

*Your life span
as a
human being is
short and fast
so when you
have an
opportunity to
enjoy yourself
you definitely
should not
waist the
chance*

The people who are not your friends are not your friends and don't you forget it

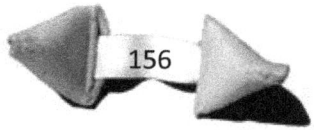

*Progress
payments,
where
and
what
are
yours*

Your biggest concern should be your future

158

*When your
success involves
the help of
other people; it
is very
important to
understand how
those people
think
because then
you will know
how to appeal to
them*

The end

Additional books written by
Dr. Kareem Pottinger available online at
www.FORTUNECOOKIES.me
and your local book stores nationwide

FORTUNE COOKIES VOLUMES 1-11

   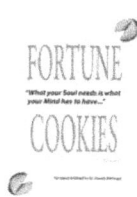

also   available   on   your

Kindle   Nook   Apple   devices